TIGERS CAN'T PURR!
AND OTHER AMAZING FACTS

By Thea Feldman
Illustrated by Lee Cosgrove

Ready-to-Read

SIMON SPOTLIGHT

An imprint of Simon & Schuster Children's Publishing Division • New York London Toronto Sydney New Delhi
1230 Avenue of the Americas, New York, New York 10020 • This Simon Spotlight edition July 2020 • Text and illustrations copyright
© 2020 Simon & Schuster, Inc. Stock photos by iStock. All rights reserved, including the right of reproduction in whole or in part in any form.
SIMON SPOTLIGHT, READY-TO-READ, and colophon are registered trademarks of Simon & Schuster, Inc. For information about special discounts
for bulk purchases, please contact Simon & Schuster Special Sales at 1-866-506-1949 or business@simonandschuster.com. Manufactured in the
United States of America 0620 LAK 10 9 8 7 6 5 4 3 2 1 Library of Congress Cataloging-in-Publication Data Names: Feldman, Thea, author.
Cosgrove, Lee, illustrator. Title: Tigers can't purr! : and other amazing facts / by Thea Feldman ; illustrations by Lee Cosgrove. Description: New
York : Simon Spotlight, an imprint of Simon & Schuster Children's Publishing Division, 2020. | Series: Super facts for super kids | Summary: "A
nonfiction Level 2 Ready-to-Read filled with fun facts about what makes tigers super"— Provided by publisher. Identifiers: LCCN 2019057026
ISBN 9781534467743 (trade paperback) | ISBN 9781534467750 (hardcover) | ISBN 9781534467767 (eBook)
Subjects: LCSH: Tiger—Miscellanea—Juvenile literature. | Children's questions and answers. Classification: LCC QL737.C23 F3958
2020 DDC 599.756—dc23 LC record available at https://lccn.loc.gov/2019057026

GLOSSARY

apex predator: an animal who is not eaten or hunted by other animals in the wild

camouflage: when an animal uses its natural colors or traits to hide in its surroundings

chuff: to push air out through the nostrils to show excitement and greet other tigers

endangered: at risk of disappearing forever

extinct: no longer existing on Earth

grasslands: large open areas covered in grass

habitat: the natural environment where an animal lives

predator: an animal who hunts, kills, and eats other animals

prey: an animal hunted by a predator

recycled: made from materials that have been used before

retractable: able to be pulled back in

territory: an area of land that animals claim for themselves

Note to readers: Some of these words may have more than one definition. The definitions above match how these words are used in this book.

CONTENTS

Tigers are super.

They can climb tall trees

and roar as loud as jet planes.

There's one thing that tigers

cannot do, though . . . purr!

WOW!

By the time you get to the tail end of this book, you'll know all about what makes tigers amazing!

COOL!

SUPER!

CHAPTER 1

TOP HUNTERS

There are six types of tigers in the world.

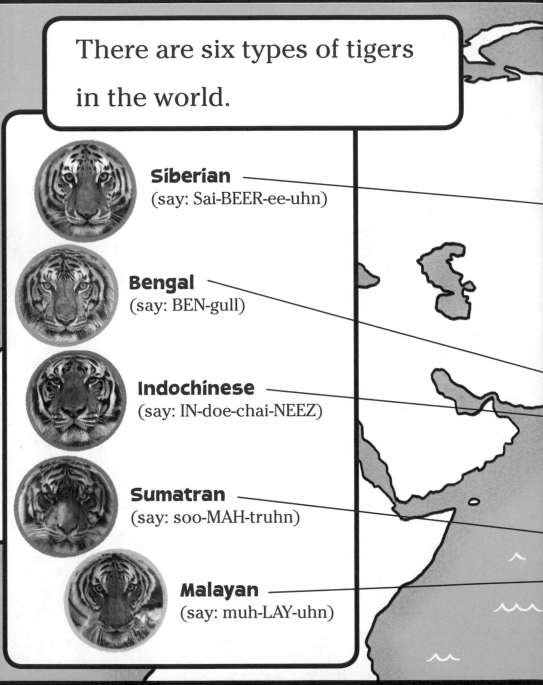

Siberian
(say: Sai-BEER-ee-uhn)

Bengal
(say: BEN-gull)

Indochinese
(say: IN-doe-chai-NEEZ)

Sumatran
(say: soo-MAH-truhn)

Malayan
(say: muh-LAY-uhn)

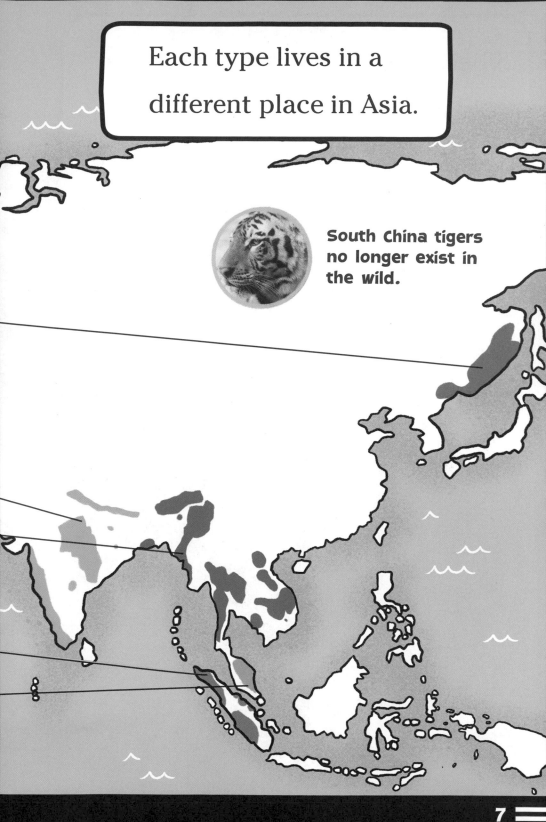

Each type lives in a different place in Asia.

South China tigers no longer exist in the wild.

Siberian tigers mostly live in cold and snowy forests.

Other tigers live in hot and swampy habitats (say: HA-bih-tats), or homes.

Some live in dry grasslands and rain forests, too.

COLD!

HOT!

DEER

WATER BUFFALO

CROCODILE

All tigers are predators
(say: PRED-uh-turz),
which means they hunt and eat
other animals called prey
(say: PRAY).
Their prey includes deer,
water buffalo, and even
other predators like crocodiles!

Tigers hunt about once a week and can eat up to 88 pounds of food when they are hungry. That is heavier than 350 bananas! They sometimes bury the leftovers and dig them up to eat later.

CHOW TIME!

Tigers are called apex (say: AY-pecks) or top predators because they aren't hunted or eaten by any other animals in the wild. For example, insects are eaten by wild pigs, who in turn are eaten by Bengal tigers. Since no one eats tigers, they are apex predators . . . one of the top hunters in the world!

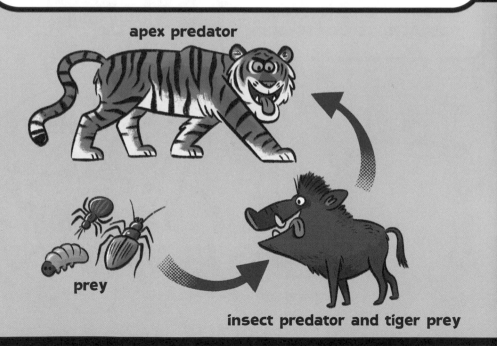

apex predator

prey

insect predator and tiger prey

CHAPTER 2

TERRIFIC FROM HEAD TO TAIL

When you imagine tigers, you probably first think of their bold stripes. Each tiger has its own pattern of stripes.

If you ever shaved a tiger's fur, you'd discover that it even has stripes on its skin!

The thin stripes help tigers blend into the thin shadows of tall grass, making it hard to spot them.

This ability to blend in and hide is called camouflage (say: KAM-uh-flahj).

Siberian tigers are bigger than any other cat in the world. They can grow up to about 10 feet long and weigh as much as 660 pounds.

That means a Siberian tiger is longer than two and a half male Great Danes . . . and heavier than five of them!

660 pounds

600 pounds

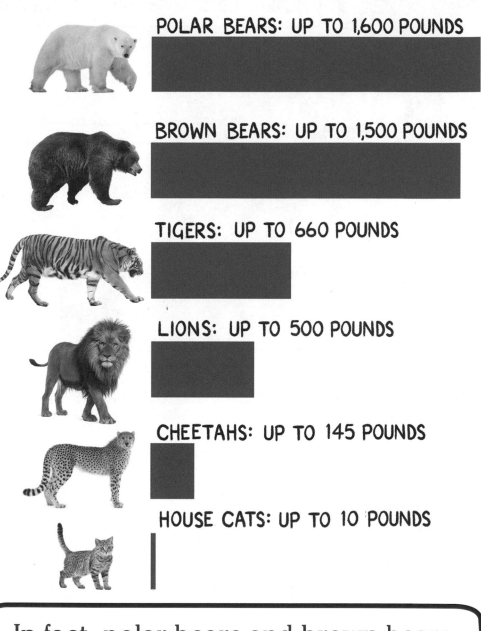

POLAR BEARS: UP TO 1,600 POUNDS

BROWN BEARS: UP TO 1,500 POUNDS

TIGERS: UP TO 660 POUNDS

LIONS: UP TO 500 POUNDS

CHEETAHS: UP TO 145 POUNDS

HOUSE CATS: UP TO 10 POUNDS

In fact, polar bears and brown bears are the only predators on land larger than Siberian tigers.

Human: up to 27.8 miles per hour

20 2 30 35 40

Tiger: up to 40 miles per hour

Don't let a tiger's large size fool you into thinking it moves slowly, though. They can run up to 40 miles per hour, which is faster than the fastest human ever!

Tigers have long hind legs, which help them push hard off the ground and leap up to 30 feet.

That's half the length of a bowling lane!

Here's something else that's terrific about tigers.

They can move very quietly, thanks to retractable claws that they can pull back into their toes.

This way, the claws don't hit against the ground and make noise when they walk.

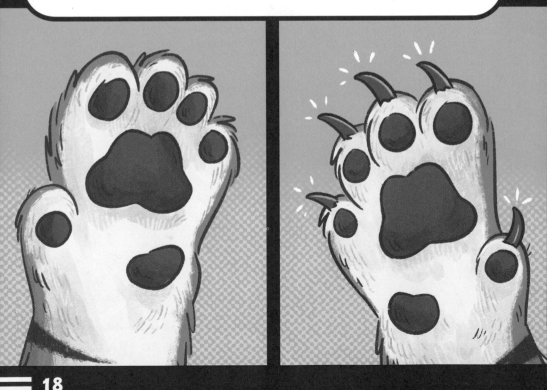

Tigers also have padding on their paws that muffle sounds.

Tigers don't see clearly for the first few weeks of their lives. But adult tigers can see about six times better in the dark than most humans.

Tigers also hear better than humans, and can turn their ears in different directions to focus on specific sounds. All these skills are helpful for tigers to catch prey!

CHAPTER 3

NOT A HOUSE CAT!

Tigers might look like giant house cats, but they differ in many ways. For example, tigers can't purr! Scientists believe tigers can't purr because of extra tissue in their throats.

PURR

ROAR

Tigers may not be able to purr . . . but they can ROAR!

Tigers also hiss, growl, groan, and grunt. Mothers moan to their cubs to get their attention. Tigers chuff to greet one another, and when they are excited.

Chuffing is when tigers close their mouths and push air out through their nostrils.

Tigers don't just "talk" to other tigers with their voices. Male tigers declare their territory, an area they want to claim as their own, by scratching their claws on trees and the ground.

They also rub their faces or spray their urine against rocks and trees in the territory.

All these marks and scents tell other tigers to "Stay away!"

EWW!

Tigers and house cats are also different when it comes to water. Most house cats hate getting wet, but tigers like it! They go into rivers and lakes to cool off.

Tigers are also great swimmers and can swim up to five miles.

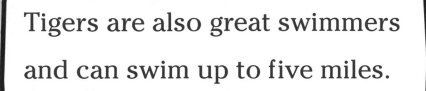

That's more than 160 laps in an Olympic pool!

One way that tigers *are* like house cats is that they both sleep a lot! Tigers sleep about 16 to 20 hours a day, mostly during the daytime.

Why do tigers snooze so much? It's a super way to store up their energy. All that hunting, roaring, and swimming takes a lot of work!

If you could have one tiger skill, what would it be?

Would you like to jump 30 feet . . .

camouflage in the grass . . .

. . . or maybe sleep 20 hours a day?

Tigers are super in so many ways, but the coolest thing about them is . . . up to you!

Turn the page to learn about why tigers are disappearing, and how you can help!

Tigers are endangered (say: en-DAYNE-jurd). That means that they are in danger of becoming extinct (say: EX-tinkt) and disappearing forever. In fact, some tiger species have already gone extinct. Scientists think that the South China tiger no longer exists in the wild, although a few still live in zoos and protected nature reserves.

There are less than 4,000 tigers left in the wild. Why? People hunt and kill tigers, even though it is illegal. They also destroy the tigers' habitats by cutting down trees or by moving onto their land.

How can you help tigers?

People cut down trees from tiger habitats to make paper products. You can use less paper by using reusable shopping bags, lunch boxes, cups, and plates. If you must use paper, look for products made from recycled paper, which are made from paper that has already been used before. Your actions can help a super tiger!